BRITAIN IN OLD PHO

Leckhampton

ALAN GILL & ERIC MILLER

for the

LECKHAMPTON LOCAL HISTORY SOCIETY

SUTTON PUBLISHING LIMITED

Sutton Publishing Limited
Phoenix Mill · Thrupp · Stroud
Gloucestershire · GL5 2BU

First published 2000

Title page: Sheepshed (or Sheepshead) Row
Cottages in Kidnappers Lane, *c.* 1910. At
the time they comprised four dwellings. By
the early 1960s they had become derelict
and were demolished, to be replaced by a
modern 'period' cottage.

British Library Cataloguing in Publication Data
A catalogue record for this book is available from the
British Library.

ISBN 0-7509-2560-4

Typeset in 10.5/13.5 Photina.
Typesetting and origination by
Sutton Publishing Limited.
Printed and bound in England by
J.H. Haynes & Co. Ltd, Sparkford.

Leckhampton Local History Society was founded in 1992. Its aims are to collect, study and publish information concerning the history of Leckhampton and to stimulate public interest in local history. It organises talks and discussions as well as outings and field trips, and there are opportunities to participate in research groups. Several books have been produced. *Leckhampton 1894 – the End of an Era* included the results of members' research into the breakup of the manorial estate, and local inhabitants also contributed reminiscences towards *Leckhampton in the Second World War*, while *Leckhampton Yesteryear* described the growth of the village and developments in everyday life during the intervening period. In 1999 the Society issued its first substantial collection of research papers, complementing its quarterly newsletter, *Smoke Signal.*

Further information about the Society's activities may be obtained from the acting Honorary Secretary, Amy Woolacott, on 01242 522566.

CONTENTS

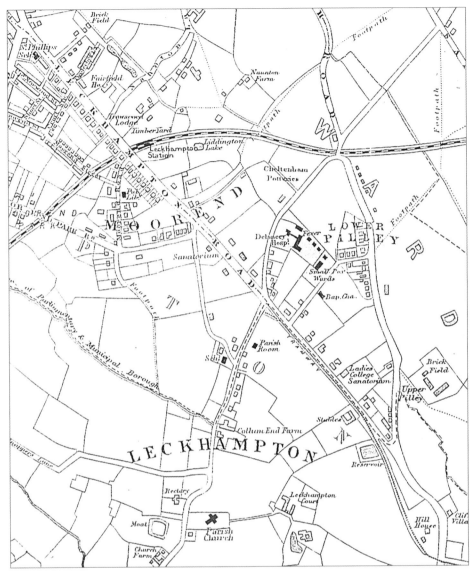

This map of 1897 shows many features of earlier Leckhampton. At the heart of the old village are the parish church, the court, the rectory and the moat, as well as the school and the newly built parish hall (marked as 'Parish Room'), all in open country. The horse-drawn tramway from the quarries still existed as far as the junction with Church Road, passing the stables and terminating at a siding where the post office now stands. As well as the sanatorium for the Ladies' College there was another lower down Leckhampton Road for the Boys' College, while the Delancey was an isolation hospital. The present-day electricity sub-station in Moorend Road is shown in its earlier incarnation as a public library (and formerly the Local Board room). The course of the Banbury & Cheltenham Direct Railway is a prominent feature near the top of the map, and close to Leckhampton station are the Liddington Lake Pleasure Gardens. The lake was formed from flooded claypits, which were among the many that provided materials for local brick fields and potteries, also marked. At the top of the map is St Philip's School. Further along Leckhampton Road, Trowscoed Lodge and Fairfield House, with its lake, stood in their own spacious grounds to the south of 'Tinderbox Lane'.

INTRODUCTION

Even though today it appears to be no more than a suburb of Cheltenham, for much of its existence Leckhampton was an entirely separate community. In the ninth century too it was an outpost of its more influential neighbour, serving as the home farm for the royal manor of Cheltenham, in common with the other nearby settlements at Charlton Kings, Prestbury and Swindon. The Anglo-Saxon name is generally held to mean 'homestead where leeks (or any kind of vegetable) are grown'. Market gardening still thrives on the fine alluvial soil of the valley, while traces of earlier ploughing can still be made out in the ridge and furrow patterns on the lower slopes of the hill, now used for grazing.

In the Domesday Survey of 1086 two manorial estates were listed under the heading of Leckhampton. One was probably centred on an island surrounded by a moat, which is still recognisable, though much overgrown with trees, beside the rectory. The other manor, whose administrative centre was on the site of Leckhampton Court, was more powerful and in due course took over the majority of the land in the area.

The lords of the manor – the inter-related families of the Giffards, the Norwoods and the Tryes – had a considerable influence over the development of the village and its consequent appearance today. Leckhampton Court, one of the oldest domestic buildings in the county, was begun by Sir John Giffard, who died in the early fourteenth century. William Norwood had the half-timbered Tudor south wing built. In the nineteenth century Charles Brandon Trye developed the limestone quarries and the tramway that linked them with Cheltenham and Gloucester; however, the financial failure of the estate led to its sale in 1894. The court is now a Sue Ryder Home, but in the intervening period it has also served as a hospital, a prisoner-of-war camp and a private school.

The tower and chancel of St Peter's church survive unchanged from the building first erected by Sir John Giffard, using local stone; the slender spire is a landmark for miles around. In the nineteenth century, to accommodate the increasing population of the area, the church was enlarged by the architect John Middleton, while another, SS Philip and James's, was built to cater for those living in the area of The Park and Upper Bath Road.

The historic parish, both civil and ecclesiastical, was comparatively large and extended from the prehistoric camp at the top of the Cotswold escarpment down to the Severn Vale. The medieval village was close to both manor house and church. The earlier layout is indicated by a few surviving seventeenth-century thatched and timber-framed cottages, one row of which probably follows the line of an old track leading away from the church and the hill. The village was sparsely inhabited until early in the nineteenth century, and its land was largely devoted to agricultural use. Such industry as existed occurred on the periphery, and some artisan dwellings near the top of Old Bath Road and in Pilley housed quarrymen and brickmakers. In general it was not until the mid- to late nineteenth century that new housing began to spread up the hill, in addition to a few scattered villas occupied by the gentry.

Schools were opened in the mid-nineteenth century, of which the National School (Leckhampton Primary) thrives today. St Philip's closed in 1908 when Naunton Park School was opened, though its building is still in use for other purposes. Improvements introduced in Queen Victoria's Diamond Jubilee year of 1897 included the village hall, which remains in constant use. The Local Board room was the seat of government of the old parish before the more populous northern part was transferred to Cheltenham Borough in 1894. Other features that gave the village its individuality included the Liddington Lake Pleasure Ground, a pottery and brick and tile works and two caravan factories; while the passenger trams and the railway station provided links to the wider world.

The parish boundaries, especially the civil and electoral ones, have changed several times in recent years. The area covered by this book therefore extends somewhat beyond the historic parish, to include Naunton Park for example; but it will correspond with what is generally regarded as pertaining to Leckhampton.

Artists and photographers over the centuries have been kind to the village. Its fine manor house and church attracted the attention of eighteenth- and nineteenth-century engravers, and Johannes Kip's distinctive 'bird's-eye' perspective, published in 1712, offers the earliest representation of both. In the heyday of picture postcard production, Leckhampton was also lucky to have its own exponent in Frank Webley, who sold a wide selection of views at a sweet shop and tobacconist's in Leckhampton Road and later at the post office. Several of the pictures are from the estate of the late Bruce Stait, a founder member of the Society, who was not only a collector but in the 1960s himself took a number of aerial photographs of the area.

The Society has altogether gathered a collection of over 500 images, many of them rare or unique. From these we have selected over 200 which we believe give the best possible rounded view of the area. Most have been donated or loaned by private individuals, others have been made available by public and private institutions, some have been copied from local newspapers and, for the sake of completeness, a small number have been reproduced from other publications. A full list of acknowledgements is given on page 128, together with a select bibliography.

While we have endeavoured to present the publishers with the sharpest possible copies of illustrations for this book, it should be pointed out that some of the originals were in poor condition, or could only be obtained as laser prints. In such cases we hope that the interest of the subject will compensate for any blemish.

Alan Gill and Eric Miller
July 2000

1

The Old Village

Collum End Farm in 1904, when it was a busy working farm, with cowsheds and cider press. The earliest parts of the building date from the late sixteenth to early seventeenth centuries. It has since been divided into two private residences.

An aerial view, looking up towards the junction of Old Bath Road and Leckhampton Road, with the escarpment of the hill beyond, 1960. The unmade Pilford Road stands out clearly to the left of Old Bath Road, and to the left of Leckhampton Road is Chatsworth Drive. Two caravan factories can be made out: the Cheltenham Caravan Company, opposite the Ladies' College sanatorium, behind which is Siddall's. The reservoir had not yet been covered over and is plainly identifiable, next to the tree-lined route of the former tramway that led down from Daisy Bank. The course of the long straight rail track that led down from the hill to Charlton Kings is also apparent.

Opposite: An aerial view taken from near the church, looking east, 1960. Church Road runs from the bottom of the picture to join Leckhampton Road, and Charlton Lane and Greenhills Road lead the eye towards Charlton Kings. The church, the rectory and the Vineries Nursery, the school playing field and the intensively cultivated allotments are prominent in the foreground, as are the concrete bases of the prisoner-of-war huts in the orchard by the avenue that leads to the court, showing how far the camp extended. The houses in Collum End Rise had not yet been built.

An aerial view of Church Road in 1960, showing the church, the Vineries Nursery, Collum End Farm, The Close and the allotments.

A mid-nineteenth-century engraving showing a view of Cheltenham from Leckhampton Hill. Artist's licence has been used in order to include a wide panorama from a point further up the road above Daisy Bank. Prominent in the foreground are the spire of Leckhampton church, Tower Lodge and a winding drum associated with the tramway that served the quarries. Leckhampton Road and Old Bath Road sweep towards the town, where various church towers and steeples stand out, with Cleeve Hill in the background.

Leckhampton St. Peter's Parish Hall.

To Major R. C. Barnard.

A GRAND BAZAAR in aid of the above Parish Hall, will be held in the MONTPELIER ROTUNDA, Cheltenham, on Tuesday, Wednesday and Thursday, November 10th, 11th and 12th.

We sincerely trust that you will help this undertaking by your presence and liberality.

A leaflet advertising the Grand Bazaar held in November 1896 to raise funds for the parish hall. In a parish magazine account of the event, Sir John Dorrington (the then-MP for Cirencester) was singled out for his 'witty speech into the Phonograph' – at that time still a great novelty. The final bill came to just over £1,238 and was paid off in 1904. Major Robert Cary Barnard, to whom the invitation is addressed, was an important and influential local personage, whom we meet again in Chapter Eight. The building of the parish hall was an important factor in cementing the sense of village identity at the end of the nineteenth century. Its creation was due very largely to the efforts of the Revd Clifford Aston, who saw it as a means of providing opportunities for communal entertainment, recreation and self-improvement. The building opened with a concert in aid of the National School on 26 April 1897 – Queen Victoria's Diamond Jubilee year – and was seen as one of the permanent memorials of her reign.

The gates of the parish hall, early 1970s. The gates, in both cast and wrought iron, are a good example of the work of William Letheren at the Vulcan Iron Works in Cheltenham, and were completed in 1901. The frame below the keys of St Peter was designed to hold a gas lamp. The Nissen hut seen in the background was used for storage, having previously seen service at the prisoner-of-war camp.

Church Road beside the parish hall, looking east, early 1930s. There was no pavement on the north side at this point, and no houses at the end of the road. Church Road is an ancient route whose medieval name was 'Collum Street', from col (either 'charcoal' or a personal name) and ham – a meadow. The road would have led to 'Collum Piece' and 'Collum Fields'. The next few pictures lead the reader from this point to the church and the south-western edge of the parish.

Cromwell Cottage, *c.* 1905. The demolition in 1962 of one of Leckhampton's oldest buildings, to be replaced by two bungalows, has been widely lamented, though it has to be admitted that there was no historical basis for its fanciful name. When auctioned in 1894 as part of the Leckhampton Court Estate, it contained two rooms up and down, together with an outside wash-house and closet. Water was obtained from the village well on the opposite side of the road.

The war memorial, shortly after being unveiled in 1920, on the site of the former village well. The names of thirty-five men who died in the First World War are engraved on a brass plaque, to which nine more have been added from the Second World War. It is still the practice to hold a short commemoration service there on Armistice Sunday. The memorial was designed by R.C. Barnard's son Leonard and was made of stone from the Leckhampton Quarry. Cromwell Cottage can be seen in the background.

Church Road under snow, from the corner of Hall Road, *c*. 1910.

Norwood Cottages, Church Road, *c.* 1910. These two thatched cottages, built of stone and timber, with an upper floor in the roof space, were advertised in the 1894 sale as each having a closet to the rear and a well, though a nearby householder also had the right to draw water from it. The building is now a single residence, 60 Church Road. It had possibly been used as a dame school in the mid-nineteenth century.

A painting of Church Road in 1824, which makes up in quaintness for what it perhaps lacks in accuracy. The church spire overlooks the scene, though the precise identity of the buildings on the left is open to speculation.

Church Road, looking east, with a row of cheerful Leckhampton children posing across the uncluttered carriageway, *c.* 1905. Brampton has more recently been given a coat of cement rendering, and its name has been transferred to the neighbouring bungalow.

Church Road, photographed from a similar viewpoint to the scene above, 1930s. The pavement has been made up on both sides of the road, which itself has been asphalted. The 30 mph signs stand close to the boundary of Cheltenham and Leckhampton.

Old Farthings, Church Road, in 1975, before it was modernised and extended. The house, dating from the early eighteenth century, had originally comprised just two rooms upstairs and two down, with a laundry and stable, a cart shed and piggeries in its grounds. The present name was inspired by the discovery of a number of old coins behind the wainscoting at the time of the restoration. The cottage had been acquired by Cecil Elwes to use as a clubhouse for his estate workers and was referred to as the Leckhampton Working Men's Club. It was also rented out to other organisations, who could take advantage of the billiard room and a shooting range in the grounds behind. The latter was still in existence during the Second World War, when it was used by the Home Guard.

Old Cottages adjacent to Collum End Farm, c. 1910. Those on the left are heavily camouflaged in ivy, which obscures the timber framing with wattle-and-daub infilling. At that time there were three separate dwellings, of which the two on the left have since been combined into one.

Collum End Farm, in the first years of the twentieth century. The sign board advertises 'Arthur Pearman, Families Supplied – Dairy Products Delivered Twice Daily to all Parts of the Town'. The Pearmans were an important family in Leckhampton at that time. Arthur Pearman was also the manager of the stone quarry, succeeding his father, Neighbour Pearman, who had in addition been the registrar and parish clerk for forty-five years until shortly before his death in 1898. Ann Pearman was the village postmistress (when the post office occupied a now demolished house at the corner of Hall Road and Church Road), while Walter Pearman was listed as a bookmaker.

A pencil sketch of Collum End Farm, 1947. As well as showing the profusion of ivy and the thick hedge, all of which have since been cleared away, this drawing is of interest for being the work of one of the German prisoners of war who were quartered at the Leckhampton Court camp, and is one of several pieces of artwork to have been given to local inhabitants who had offered hospitality. Though fraternisation between the soldiers and the local populace was discouraged at first, there was an unofficial two-way letterbox behind a loose stone in the wall of the farm. Whether as a result of these contacts or the more relaxed regime that followed, several of the soldiers married local girls and even settled in the area.

The last days of Collum End Farm, as seen from the bedroom window of Bruce Stait's house in 1960. Above are seen the farmyard and stables and below the start of construction of Collum End Rise, with the hill and the court in the distance.

Leckhampton Court Lower Lodge, 1907. Dating from the early nineteenth century, this is one of three lodges built on the approaches to the court, and its sturdy gateposts echo those at the front quadrangle of the court itself. The ivy has since been removed and the building extended.

Church Road, looking east towards the junction with Kidnappers Lane on the left, 1956. The cyclist is believed to be Alf Bendall. The trees were removed soon afterwards when the bend was straightened and the road widened.

Church Road outside the churchyard, a hundred yards further west than in the previous photograph, *c.* 1910. The narrowness of the road at this point is striking. The street lamp was one of three erected in 1907 by Captain Elwes and Canon Proctor to light the way for churchgoers on dark evenings. Note the little girl wearing a pinafore and holding a hoop.

The moat, 1866. This was probably the location of one of Leckhampton's two medieval manor houses. When the site was excavated in 1933, traces of a stone building were uncovered on the island, with access by a bridge and a fortified gateway dating from probably the fourteenth century. Though now overgrown and partly built over, the moat used to be full of water, and older inhabitants recall skating on its frozen surface.

Hall Road (above) looking towards Church Road in about 1903, before the main school building (below) wa
erected. The original National School, opened in 1841, was inadequate for twentieth-century needs, and a nev
school for juniors was opened in 1906. A further wing was added for the infants in 1931; the original ston
building remains in use as the dining hall.

A class of Leckhampton schoolchildren with their teacher, outside the old school building, probably no later than 1890. The photograph came from the collection of the late Miss Jean Bendall, whose maternal grandfather Barnard Thompson was the school's headmaster at that time (see also page 94). He lived in the school house with his wife and seven children, all of whom attended the school. His eldest daughter Edith was a pupil teacher there in 1894.

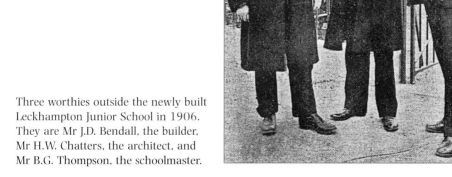

Three worthies outside the newly built Leckhampton Junior School in 1906. They are Mr J.D. Bendall, the builder, Mr H.W. Chatters, the architect, and Mr B.G. Thompson, the schoolmaster.

A class of girls at Leckhampton School when the new school building was opened, 1906. Back row, left to right: Edith Allen, Bertha Ursell, Hilda Turner, Alice Ballinger, Gertie Little, Eva Everett. Third row: Gladys Little, Grace Hunt, Minnie Burford, Rose Bubb, Lizzie Fordham, Lily Matthews, Elsie Chick, Kittie Robinson. Second row: Evelyn Whittle, Kate Dewing (?), Leah Dance, May Smith, Elsie Mustoe, Winnie Everett, Jennie James, Esther Dance. Front row: Edith Field, Mabel Williams, Molly Cotton, Ethel Townsend, Nelly Barrett, Lily Little, Dot Harper.

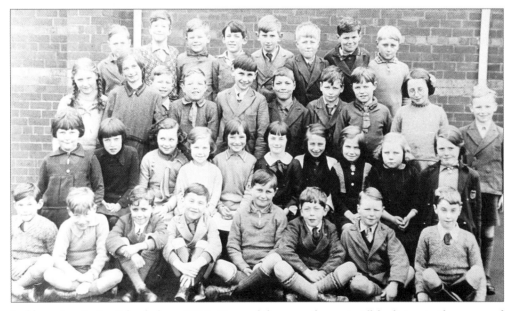

Leckhampton Junior School class, 1935. Many of these pupils must still be living in the area and they are invited to provide some of the names.

2

The Court

The north wing of Leckhampton Court, *c.* 1910. It is this side of the building that is seen from Church Road by passers-by. Ivy masks the nineteenth-century 'Tudorbethan' façade and the oriel window at the end of the banqueting hall, above a formal terrace. At this time the much older part at the extreme right, with its twisted brick chimneys, was used as the chapel.

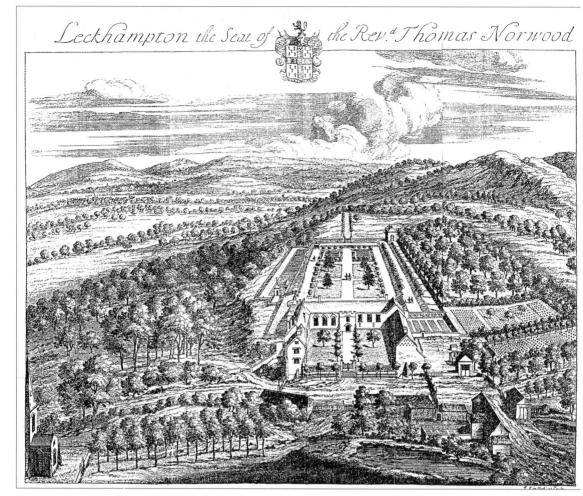

An engraving of Leckhampton Court by Johannes Kip, taken from *The Ancient and Present State of Gloucestershire* published in 1712. This, the first ever representation of the court, is characteristic of Kip's fanciful 'bird's-eye' views of the country residences of Britain, designed to flatter the owner – in this case the Revd Thomas Norwood who was also rector of St Peter's church, which Kip has squeezed into the bottom left-hand corner of the drawing. The general layout of the house and grounds is still identifiable today, including the avenue of trees leading down to the church, the lake in the foreground next to the stables, the vegetable garden and even what resembles a 'Tudor garage' to the right of the main building. However, the steps in front of the gates to the front quadrangle have been repositioned below the main entrance.

These engravings show further stages in the growth of Leckhampton Court. The first, from Samuel Lysons's *Collection of Gloucestershire Antiquities* published in 1793, clearly shows some semi-circular front steps and William Norwood's south wing. The rather bleak rectangular building in the left-hand corner of the quadrangle, abutting the banqueting hall, was built after a fire in 1732 had destroyed part of the north wing. A space remained between it and the three-storey building at the left of the picture. The second engraving (below) is taken from *A New Historical Description of Cheltenham*, published in 1826. By then the steps had been moved, but the Georgian stop-gap was still standing. In 1841 the property was put up for sale by Henry Norwood Trye, who had run into serious financial difficulties, and was bought by his brother, the Revd Charles Brandon Trye. In due course he had that part demolished but added the window at the exposed end of the banqueting hall and a covered arcade at the front. So it remained until John Hargreaves acquired the court after the great sale of the estate in 1894, and had the north wing built.

William Norwood, from an oil painting, 1619. This portrait, by an unknown artist, hangs in Cheltenham Art Gallery and shows the Lord of the Manor of Leckhampton at the age of seventy-one. Among his distinctions, he had been High Sheriff of the county and, for a time, Lord of the Manor of Cheltenham through his marriage to Elizabeth Lygon, of Madresfield, to whom he dedicated a memorial brass in the church. Improvements to the court were carried out by him, including the construction of the timber-framed south wing, at whose eastern end is a doorway bearing the date 1582.

Leckhampton Court, from *Norman's History of Cheltenham*, published in 1863. This view shows the building which was erected after the fire in 1732, above an idealised pastoral scene. The only recognisable feature is the Tudor annexe to the right, with its twisted brick chimneys.

A view from the drive leading from Tower Lodge towards the court, with the church in the distance. Dated 1863, it is the earliest known photograph of Leckhampton.

The main entrance to Leckhampton Court, *c.* 1911. This courtyard was the scene of entertainments during many village fêtes. In 1898, for example, it was turned into an 'oriental bazaar', in which – as reported in the parish magazine – 'many pretty and charming ladies dispensed their various wares'. In 1906 Captain and Mrs Elwes invited the whole village there to celebrate their fifth wedding anniversary and the births of their two children. Over 300 adults sat down to a meal, followed later by the same number of children.

Captain Cecil Elwes, Mrs Muriel Elwes and their two children, 1906. The children's baptismal names – Cecilia Muriel Hargreaves and John Hargreaves – are a reminder that Mrs Elwes was herself the second daughter of John Hargreaves.

The banqueting hall of Leckhampton Court in 1884, when John Hargreaves already occupied it as a tenant. The wood panelling obscures the windows facing on to the lawn to the left. The room is decorated in High Victorian manner, with family portraits and decorative plates and scarcely a surface not covered. Above the door a large canvas of a huntsman covers the minstrels' gallery.

The gardens on the east side of Leckhampton Court, *c.* 1910. They were clearly well stocked and cared for, reminiscent of the elaborate parterres shown earlier in the drawing by Kip. The ivy-covered gable on the left is at the end of the Tudor wing built by William Norwood.

The entrance to Leckhampton Court during the First World War. A notice board indicates that it was in use as a hospital, run by a Voluntary Aid Detachment of the Red Cross. Some 1,700 wounded British, Australian, Canadian and Belgian servicemen were patients there, with only two deaths recorded, neither of them from their wounds.

The drawing room in the newly built north wing of Leckhampton Court, *c.* 1896, with oriental carpets hung on the walls and draped over chairs; note the aspidistra. The photograph was taken by Helen de Lacy Lacy, a friend of John Hargreaves's daughter Muriel. Her name was mentioned in January 1899 in an account in the *Cheltenham Looker-on* as having performed in some *tableaux vivants* ('living pictures', in which the performers remain motionless and represent a well-known painting), organised by Muriel Hargreaves to raise money for the parish hall. The orientalia would have been collected by John Hargreaves during his travels, and some of them were displayed at village fêtes.

The same room during the First World War, converted for use as a hospital ward. The patients were taught basket-work, drawing and embroidery to aid their recuperation. The piano, seen in front of the fire-place, would have been used in Sunday evening concerts, to which patients and staff contributed.

The Leckhampton Court Hospital patients and staff, 20 December 1918. This photograph was taken on the return of the Commandant, Mrs Grace Ward, from Buckingham Palace where she had received the MBE from the King. She is seated in the middle of the front row.

Orderlies photographed in 1919 before the hospital was closed down. They represent only about half the total number who served there. Back row, left to right: W. Wells, G. Bellamy, G. Hawker, C. Richings, a visitor, J. Carter, P. Williams, W. Leach, W. Yeandle. Middle row: R.E. Whiting, C. Roberts, G. Fordham, C. Hall, H. Sperring, W.J. Scaldwell, W. Murphy, T.W. Mott. Front row: J. Holman, R.H. Saunders, P.H. Beddard, R.H. Kenworthy, H.S. Marshall, E. Colwell, J. Bendall, J. Aston.

Convalescing patients in fancy dress for a concert performance, 1915. Concerts and fêtes were organised in the grounds during the summer to raise money, which was spent on luxuries not provided for by the official War Office allowance. This photograph was taken by Frank Webley and published in the *Graphic*. Frank Webley was himself one of the hospital orderlies.

Monument to Cecil Elwes's horse, in a field above Leckhampton Court, 1938. The inscription is now hard to make out but originally read:

TO THE MEMORY OF
THE CONTINENTAL
BY BOULEVARD-FAIRHAVEN
FOALED 1891 DIED 1902
WINNER OF 25 STEEPLECHASES
AND THE FAVOURITE HUNTER
OF CECIL ELWES
BY WHOM THESE STONES WERE ERECTED

Captain Elwes was a keen huntsman and formed his own pack of hounds in 1904, loaned by the Berkeley Hunt. It is probably these hounds that can be seen in the photograph on page 55.

3

The Churches

Leckhampton church, an engraving by G.P. Johnson, taken from *Norman's History of Cheltenham*, 1863. This view shows St Peter's as it must have appeared for over 500 years, with its characteristic tower and spire. Three years later the architect John Middleton lengthened the nave and south aisle, raised the roof level, added a new north aisle and repositioned the porch.

A lithograph of Leckhampton church by George Rowe, *c.* 1840. This view, taken from the south, shows how much smaller the building was than it is today. The vestry can just be made out, erected in 1834 by the Revd Charles Brandon Trye, in which to hold parish meetings.

A wintry view of the west end of the church, 1914.

A view of the church and its surroundings, taken during a balloon flight in 1991. The church and the churchyard, the glebe cottages, the rectory and Church Farm are clearly seen, and the ridge and furrow pattern in Church Meadow is shown up in the evening light.

A view from the top of the church spire, looking north-east over Church Road, 1971. In that year substantial repairs were carried out on the tower and spire, at the same time as the bells were rehung. The captain of the belfry, Eric Taylor, availed himself of the builders' scaffolding to take a number of panoramic photographs. This one shows Church Road in the centre of the picture and the fields beyond, which the Leckhampton Green Land Action Group (LEGLAG) seeks to protect from further development.

The interior of the church, c. 1902. Many features have been altered or removed since then, for example the reredos to the high altar, the memorial tablets, the triangular wall-brace behind the simple pulpit, the gas lighting and the heating stove.

The grave of William Fraser McDonell, VC, buried in 1894. He was one of the few civilian holders of the Victoria Cross, which he was awarded for gallantry in 1857 during the Indian Mutiny as a member of the Bengal Civil Service. He saved the lives of thirty-five men who were crossing a river under heavy fire from mutineers when a rope became entangled in the rudder. Though already wounded, in full view of the enemy he cut the rope and safely guided the boat to the other side. After retirement from his service in India as a tax collector and magistrate, he returned to Cheltenham where he had been born and educated. He successfully stood for election as a town councillor. Two other holders of the Victoria Cross are also buried at Leckhampton.

three wooden crosses commemorating men who lost their lives in the First World War. They are Alfred W.G. Enoch and Alfred Frederick Victor Hunt who died in battle, and Harold Summers who died of wounds. These crosses, which are likely to have been the original grave markers sent back from Flanders, eventually became rotten and have since been replaced with more substantial ones made of oak. The name on the one in front is Lance-Corporal A.W.G. Enoch MM, whose portrait is shown below.

Lance-Corporal Alfred William George Enoch. He was killed during the capture of Ovillers on the Somme on 21 July 1916, aged twenty-four, and was awarded the Military Medal for bravery in the field. He is commemorated on the Thiepval Memorial. He lived at Camden, Croft Street, Leckhampton, and served in the 5th Battalion of the Gloucestershire Regiment.

The Revd Clifford Aston, *c.* 1904. Clifford Aston was curate-in-charge at St Peter's from 1895 until his death in 1904. He was keen to encourage a sense of village community, and many new societies – religious, cultural, social and sporting – were formed during his incumbency. It is appropriate that a plaque was placed to his memory in the parish hall. His father had been vicar of St Luke's.

The Leckhampton Society of Change Ringers, 1923. Left to right: W. Harrison, J. Ballinger, G. Orchard (from Painswick), W. Hunt, T. Hunt (captain), ? Caudle, G. Walters, W. Townsend, F. Pratt, F. Walters, A. Hunt. These were an outstandingly loyal team and were largely the same as in 1904, when two new bells were hung, making a ring of eight. William Harrison (far left) was appointed as verger and sexton in 1923.

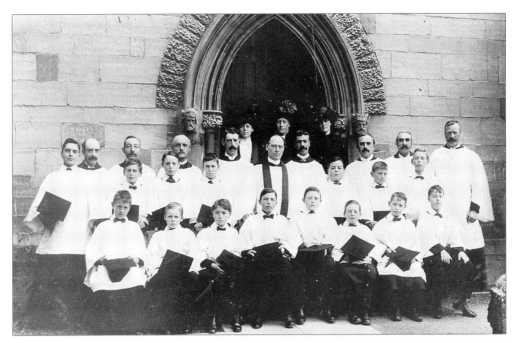

The choir of St Peter's, probably 1910.

The Rogationtide blessing of the crops procession passing in front of Leckhampton Court, *c.* 1952. The cross is carried by Reg Read and the rector is the Revd Eric Cordingly, flanked by the churchwardens Mr H.G. Poulton and Mr T.A.D. Clark. This ceremony was performed regularly each spring until the early 1950s. The procession passed from the church to the terrace of the court, led by churchwardens, clergy, and choir, followed by the various church societies and brought up in the rear by the rest of the congregation.

The clergy and choir of St Peter's, 1931. Back row, left to right: R. Read, B. Jenkins, H. Greening, F. Mitchell, A.S. Jenkins, P. Brunsdon. Third row: A. Brown, W. Townsend, R. Cooper, T. Heming, E.H. Parsons, W.E. Leech, F.W. Oakey, S.H. Jenkins, W. Harrison (verger). Scond row: Miss E.M. Robinson, Miss O. Robinson, Captain J.H. Trye, RN, (churchwarden), Canon F.W. Sears (rector), H. Latimer Taylor (churchwarden), A.W. Barradell (organist), Miss Weaver, Miss Earée. Front row: H. Smith, B. Hewer, R. Sollars, L. Jenkins, N. Burrows, R. Davison, C. Lewis. Mr Parsons was the headmaster of Leckhampton Primary School. Captain Trye was later elected as Mayor of Cheltenham.

St Peter's Young Wives group, 1952. Back row, left to right: Mmes Millichip, Moodie, Webb, -?-, the Revd Eric Cordingly (rector), Mmes Jillings, Robertson, Jukes. Second row: Mmes Vernon, -?-, -?-, Barrett, Foster, Taylor, Gwither, Williams, Smith, Edmonds. Third row: Mmes -?-, -?-, Lea, Townsend, -?-, Davis, -?-, -?-, -?-, -?-. Front row: Mmes Launchbury, Mikeson, Evans, Townley, Cordingly, Jones, Newcombe, Marlow, Leeding. Several of the ladies are still active in the parish as members of the Mothers' Union.

An engraving of the first SS Philip and St James's church (originally known as simply St Philip's) by G.P. Johnson, shortly after its construction in 1840. By the middle of the nineteenth century Leckhampton's population had increased ten-fold, and this church was designed to cater for the new inhabitants living in 'South Town' and The Park. It remained the daughter church of St Peter's until 1869, when the parish of SS Philip and James was created. This original 'Regency Gothic' church was replaced in 1882 by the present larger and more substantial building.

Members of the Pilley Band of Hope who took part in a concert in November 1908. They are standing in front of the Pilley 'Zion' Baptist church, whose foundation stone had been laid in 1879. The children in the first and second rows – the girls in white dresses and sashes, the boys in knee-breeches and pill-box hats – include performers representing the 'town crier' and the 'fairy queen'. In the back row are Messrs Charles W. Barrett, E. Wilson and C. Hawker. No fewer than eleven other members of the Barrett family took part. Mr Barrett, of Old Bath Road, known as the 'Bishop of Pilley' because of his long connection with the Baptist church, was chairman of the band, and Mr Wilson acted as concert accompanist. Programmes of entertainment included songs and recitations ('Raise the Banner,' 'The Pawnbroker's Shop,' 'The Curfew Must not Ring Tonight,' 'Throw out the Life Line'), as well as lantern views.

Emmanuel church after its destruction in a fire, 1916. The corrugated-iron structure was lined with pitch pine, which was rapidly consumed before the horse-drawn fire appliance could complete the journey from the engine house in St James's Square. This particular church stood near the junction of Exmouth Street and Naunton Terrace and had been erected in 1872, originally as a mission hall for St Luke's. It had also suffered a disaster in 1878, when it fell down during a heavy snowstorm. After the fire, worship was carried on in an old school (now demolished) in Naunton Terrace.

Design for a proposed new Emmanuel church, 1919. The name Emmanuel recalls the church at Clifton where the Revd J.A. Aston, the vicar of St Luke's, had formerly been a curate. This gothic-style church, planned for a site in Naunton Lane, in the grounds of the demolished Trowscoed Lodge, was one of several unfulfilled attempts to create a building more properly suited to the purpose. Various other sites were mooted until the present church, of more modest proportions, was built in Fairfield Parade in 1937.

4

The Newer Areas

A No. 3 bus at the Norwood Arms in the 1930s: a paradise for cyclists, and nothing to impede the bus. Note the advertisements on the garden wall of the public house for the Daffodil and the newly built Gaumont Palace cinemas. The numbering of the Leckhampton bus route was established very early in the life of the Cheltenham Omnibus Company, in the days of horse traction; by the 1970s the Cheltenham services had been amalgamated with other services of the Bristol Tramways and Carriage Company, and the Leckhampton route had become the 590.

The tram stop at the Norwood Arms, *c.* 1905. It shows the drinking trough for horses and dogs, which was presented in 1884 by the Cheltenham Ladies' Society for the Protection of Animals. A sign advertises the Norwood Brewery; this would have been in competition with the Grafton Brewery, another small-scale brewhouse only a few hundred yards away.

The end of the 'scenic route' at the bottom of Leckhampton Road, probably in the 1960s. In the pavement outside The Norwood (formerly the Norwood Arms) are two sets of metal rails, which are a recurring source of puzzlement to observant passers-by and have often been assumed to be relics of the old mineral tramway. There are many arguments against this (not least that that section of the track was taken up in 1861), but this photograph showing the position of the gentlemen's underground toilets points to the alternative, down-to-earth explanation. These and the ladies' toilets (seen in the photograph on the previous page) line up with the rails, which will have served as frames for the glass roof that let daylight into the area beneath.

The Norwood Arms, *c.* 1900. The top storey was removed in the 1960s, when the public house was modernised. The establishment dates back to the early nineteenth century and its ales were supplied to the weary folk taking part in the traditional beating of the parish bounds, for whom it was a stopping place. Churchwardens' accounts for the 1830s list 'expenses attending perambulation' paid to its landlord, for example '7 gallons of beer (at 3*d* a pint) – 14 shillings,' 'bread and cheese,' and '18 glasses of grog – 13 shillings and sixpence'.

The Norwood Arms Pleasure Garden, 1927. A caption to this photograph in the *Gloucestershire Graphic* states that Mr P.J. Kilminster had opened the lawn of the public house as a pleasure garden and that large numbers of people were taking advantage of the beautiful spot to spend a pleasant evening with their families. Swings and a see-saw were provided for the children, and drinks were served from the 'picturesque pavilion'.

The Leckhampton Inn on Shurdington Road in a less frantic age and (below) in 1998. The three-wheeled Morgan sports car (and probably the photograph) date from the early 1920s. The rough stonework on the side walls of the inn will have been supplied from the Leckhampton Quarries by means of the tramway which passed close by. It is also apparent on the neighbouring house, the Leckhampton Inn Garage, which was later demolished though the site is still associated with the motor business. In the earlier picture the inn is advertised as being the meeting place of the RAOB, the Royal Antediluvian Order of Buffaloes.

Tombs and Company grocery stores on Shurdington Road, c. 1910. Although claiming to have been established in 1882 the business was not at this location until 1910. The site is now occupied by the Norwood Fish Bar, shown in the lower photograph.

Leckhampton Hall, 1967. It stood at the corner of Shurdington Road and Moorend Park Road and has been replaced by a block of flats. The building was empty and had been vandalised when this picture was taken. It had ten bedrooms, three acres of gardens and stabling for four horses.

A pair of houses in Croft Street – now Croft Villas – being built by Edmund Capper. *c.* 1885. Edmund Capper is standing on top of the left-hand bay and the boy holding a saw is his son Charles (the father of the late Geoff Capper). The ridge that projects above the roof tiles is a continuation of the dividing wall between the semi-detached houses, as required by local building and fire regulations at that time. This has since been removed.

Ferncliff in Moorend Crescent, home of the Capper family, *c.* 1900. As a sideline to running the building business, they also kept a shop in which they sold home-made produce. The display window can be seen on the right.

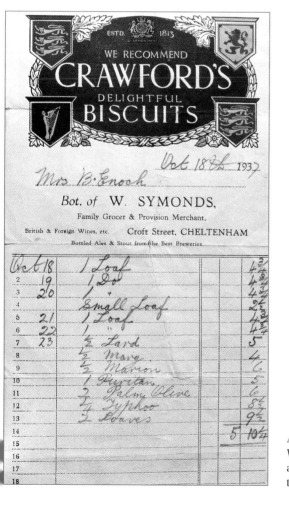

A bill from the grocer's shop on Croft Street, W. Symonds, in 1937. A large loaf of bread cost 4¾d and a small one 2½d, prices which remained stable throughout the war years.

Leckhampton station, with the bridge carrying Leckhampton Road behind. The date is unknown but must have been later than 1902, when the second platform on the left was added. The station was opened in 1881 on the line built for the Banbury and Cheltenham Direct Railway. This was taken over in 1897 by the Great Western Railway, which extended the platforms to accommodate through expresses between Cheltenham and Southampton, via Cirencester and Swindon.

Leckhampton station with staff posed for the photograph with a light engine behind, *c.* 1900. The bench support has the motif of the Midland and South Western Junction Railway (MSWJR), which also ran trains along the line.

Leckhampton station, in the early years of the twentieth century.

Leckhampton station, probably not long before its closure in 1962.

The overgrown station site, from the road bridge after the line had been closed. The track has been taken up but the platforms can still be made out. Apartments and a small industrial estate were eventually built here.

The tram passing place in Leckhampton Road, just above Hall Road, looking towards the hill, 1906.

Riders and hounds in Leckhampton Road, just below the Malvern Inn, *c*. 1900. These are presumably the hounds that were kennelled at Leckhampton Court. Foxhunting was (or was presumed to be) a prominent pastime for its occupants. For example, when the court was advertised for auction in 1841, one of the selling points was the fact that a sportsman would be within easy reach of Lord Seagrave's, the Duke of Beaufort's and Lord Dulcie's Fox Hounds, with a crack pack of stag hounds upon alternate days'.

The Leckhampton Road and Church Road junction, *c*. 1910. This view shows the post office and grocery stores run by E. Haward and the sweet shop and tobacconist's run by F.A. Webley, who published his own postcards of Leckhampton. Mr Webley later took over the post office. The photograph is also of particular interest for the rare sight of the two-tier drinking fountain (the top one for humans, the other for animals) surmounted by a lamp. This memorial of Queen Victoria's Diamond Jubilee year, 1897, was described in the parish magazine as a 'most useful present shortly to adorn the parish. . . . Standing opposite the Malvern Inn it will prove a real boon to wayfarers, both four-legged and two. It is to be hoped that the Corporation of Cheltenham will give back freely through this source some of the water they take from the hill.' The fountain was removed in 1949.

A horse-drawn omnibus outside the Malvern Inn, 1890s. The service from St James's station to the Malvern via the High Street began in 1890. The photograph below, which shows the inn exactly a hundred years later, is already part of history, as the pub has now been turned into a private house, 164 Leckhampton Road. In the process its bay window and matching porch have been removed, so that it has reverted to its earlier appearance. The inn sign in this photograph depicts the tower of Malvern Priory (which in its early days would have been visible, unobscured by houses) against a backdrop of the Malvern Hills, with post-horns and orbs in the corners. This sign was later replaced by an artistic landscape showing the view along the summit of the hills. A plaque has been set on the wall of the renovated house stating that it was a meeting place for the marchers campaigning for free access to Leckhampton Common. A newspaper account describes how in 1902 the marchers' leader made a rousing speech to an excited crowd outside the inn before they continued up the hill to carry out their vengeance.

wo views of Leckhampton Road taken from almost the same position, the top one in about 1900 and the bottom
ne in the 1930s. In 1900 the trees were newly planted and there were no buildings on the west side. The
pening into Pilley Lane can be seen beside the lamp-post on the left-hand side. A quarry truck and part of the
oneyard can be made out on the right, where houses (and the post office) were built later.

The Leckhampton Road Garage, on the corner of Pilley Lane, rebuilt in 1937. The drawing in this advertisement is a real period piece, with the art déco frontage of the showroom, the streamlined touring car on the ramp, the row of tall petrol pumps and the neat semi-detached houses behind. The garage, trading as the Leckhampton Motor Service, was owned by Mr Victor Nicholls, who specialised in reconditioning and selling reliable secondhand cars. He had also taken over the Austin agency. His son – christened Austin – trained as a garage mechanic but has also produced beautiful ornamental wrought ironwork.

The Ladies' College sanatorium, Leckhampton Road, in September 1939. It was built in 1877 and was originally intended for girls suffering from scarlet fever, typhoid and diphtheria. Miss Beale, the college principal, often went there during school holidays for rest and fresh air. The building was demolished in the 1960s to make way for Liddington Close.

Just look at this luxuriously fitted interior!

Before You Make Your All-Important Decision BE SURE TO SEE THE
CHELTENHAM RANGE

The The Eland (part interior of which is illustrated) is designed for all-the-year use. It includes a full-size gas cooker, running hot and cold water and a full-size bath.

CHELTENHAM CARAVAN Co. Ltd.
Maida Vale Works, Naunton-lane & 205 Leckhampton Rd.
'Phone Cheltenham 3572.

Miss PAT HYDE the well-known singer and B.B.C. star with her
"SIDDALL" Caravan

This attractive 'SUNSET' MODEL, panelled in figured walnut and fitted with a coal fire, is one of many styles designed and built in Cheltenham for world markets by—-

SIDDALL CARAVANS
343 OLD BATH RD., CHELTENHAM. TEL. 4618

Advertisements for caravans manufactured in Leckhampton, 1938. The choice of Pat Hyde to advertise Siddall's caravans was particularly appropriate. A musical journal of that day reports that during the summer, when travelling to engagements, this 'croonette' would travel in a smart American car pulling a caravan, which was heated by a coal fire; clearly, she favoured the Siddall 'Sunset' model, whose chimney is conspicuous in this photograph. The Cheltenham Caravan Company made use of war surplus materials to produce its first caravans in the 1920s, some of them being motorised, and by 1933, when a national caravan rally was staged at Cheltenham racecourse, the company was awarded second place in the four-berth class. During the Second World War its factory made aircraft parts. Afterwards it manufactured washing machines and for a time its range of caravans remained popular. However, the company ceased trading in 1975.

A cottage in Leckhampton Road, c. 1910. It is situated just above the Ladies' College sanatorium, which can be seen on the left. The mock-Tudor timber cladding on the cottage has since been removed.

The Leckhampton passenger tram terminus ('Foot of the Hill'), probably in 1905. Here the rails ran parallel to the quarry tramway. The track descended along Bottom Incline before passing beside Tramway Cottages, whose roof can be seen above the hedge. The cottages (not to be confused with the 'Tramway Cottage' erected by H.J. Dale) were demolished in about 1960 and made way for an electricity substation.

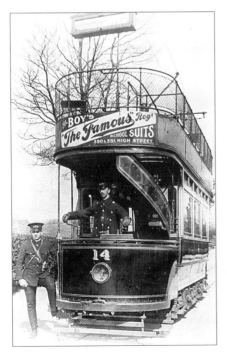

Tram No. 14 at the Leckhampton terminus, probably shortly after the introduction of trams on this route in 1905.

The Hill Stores at the junction of Leckhampton Road and Old Bath Road, *c.* 1900. There appears to be some sort of shelter at the back, presumably for those partaking of refreshments. Older inhabitants also recall a cobbler's shop there. The gas lamp is similar to the one shown near the church in the photograph on page 21. The advertisements will strike a chord, while motorists will have had to be extremely keen-sighted if they were to spot the invitation at the 'Speed Gate' to 'Drive slowly through town'.

On Easter Monday 1973 a coach attempting to climb the hill ran back and crashed into the Hill Stores, causing some damage and wrecking a postbox, but nobody was injured. Arthur Keen, the shopkeeper, is seen holding the 'Cheltenham' sign. The shop closed three years later and was replaced by a private house.

The road up Leckhampton Hill in the 1930s. The incline will have taxed the engines of that era, though not as much as it did the horses, for whom both ascent and descent would have been difficult, especially in icy conditions.

Tower Lodge, the upper lodge to Leckhampton Court, from a lithograph by Henry Lamb, *c.* 1830. At the time this drawing was made, the building served as an ale-house, known as 'Hamletts'. In 1938 it was linked with a notorious unsolved crime. Coinciding with the suicide of an occupant of the lodge, a headless torso was discovered at Haw Bridge on the River Severn. The body was believed to be that of one Captain Butt, whose bloodstained coat was found by police under floorboards at the lodge. All this provoked much local gossip and speculation, but in the absence of conclusive evidence no official cause of death could be established nor any culprit be named.

Bartlow on Leckhampton Hill, built in 1868 for Robert Cary Barnard to a design by John Middleton. This fine example of that architect's work, ornamented in contrasting red and dark grey brick, with stone mullioned windows, sadly had to be demolished a century later because of subsidence. The house was named after a village in Cambridgeshire where the family had formerly lived.

Delancey Hospital in Charlton Lane in 1898, another building designed by John Middleton. It was opened in 1874 and is named after Miss Susan Delancey, who donated £5,000 for the building of a hospital for fever or other infectious diseases; the most common cases were of smallpox, scarlet fever and diphtheria. In 1950, under the National Health Service, it was decided in view of the decline in infectious diseases to concentrate on providing accommodation for the elderly sick, and other changes and additions to the facilities have been made since then.

The Cotswold Potteries, 1908. It is hard now to imagine this industrial operation, with its bottle kiln and pall of smoke, near the site of today's Cheshire Home on Charlton Lane. The firm was in business from about 1895 to 1912 and was run by Arthur Godwin, a member of a family of Herefordshire tile-makers. The wide range of pots which he manufactured, both large and small, can be made out in the photograph (below) of a trade display, probably set out in the Winter Gardens, Imperial Square. Though the factory was dismantled long ago, Arthur Godwin's home, the red-brick Victoria House, remained until 1991, having served for a time as an office for the Health Authority. When this building was being demolished, the workmen discovered under the floorboards a large quantity of earthenware pots, which must have lain untouched since the closure of the pottery. Bricks and tiles as well as pottery were produced in the Leckhampton area for many years, the works gradually progressing up the hill as clay deposits became exhausted.

5

The Hill: Quarries, Recreation & Riots

A view of Cheltenham from Leckhampton Hill, *c.* 1908. Hill House, Ashmeade, and Ashmeade Lodge can be seen in the foreground. Pilford Brickworks with its chimney is on the right and the Ladies' College sanatorium is in the centre. Large tracts of Leckhampton are not yet built on, and the extent of cultivated land is clearly to be seen.

Cheltenham from the Devil's Chimney in 1892, a classic view of the town before the growth of its suburbs. The Devil's Chimney is a pillar of harder rock, left by quarrymen and later strengthened; little did they know that it was to become a distinctive emblem of Cheltenham! It also symbolises the competing claims of industry and leisure, which were brought to a head when the quarry owner, Henry J. Dale, attempted to deny access to the public.

An unusual view of the Devil's Chimney, looking down on Craigside Cottage and Hill Grange, date unknown. Trees now obscure this view.

The quarry below the Top Incline, 1911. Top Incline was one of several stretches of railway track which enabled stone to be carried in wagons down the hill. In the distance is the bonfire being built to celebrate the Coronation of George V.

A winding drum on the Bottom Incline with a horse-drawn quarry truck, date unknown. A loaded wagon was able to pull up an empty one, linked to the winding drum, by means of gravity. Between the Middle and Bottom Inclines the trucks were pulled by horses. The supports for the winding drum survive today.

HEARD AT LECKHAMPTON.
FOND MOTHER : Tommy, I've been looking for you; where have you been?
TOMMY (triumphant): O! only up on the Hill to down Dale!

A cartoon that appeared in the *Graphic* in March 1902, evoking the fierce resistance of the inhabitants of Leckhampton – and of Cheltenham too – against Henry Dale's action in fencing off the quarries, thereby obstructing traditional rights of way across the hill. A large crowd had assembled on the hill and partially destroyed the fences. The drawing is also of interest in that it gives the only known representation of the original Wheatsheaf Inn on Old Bath Road, which was used as an unofficial headquarters by the protesters.

The protests continued, and on 7 July 1902 a crowd estimated at around two thousand marched again to the hill. Four working men, who came to be known as the 'Leckhampton stalwarts', were charged with obstructing the police, but were acquitted on this occasion.

Tramway Cottage, which had been built across the paths and which provoked the anger of the protesters in July 1902.

A carefully posed photograph showing the destruction of the fences.

Two stages in the demolition of Tramway Cottage, 15 July 1902. On seeing the mob approach, the quarry foreman and his family fled. The house was ransacked and the building razed to the ground. In 1906 Dale rebuilt the house on the same spot, and on Good Friday 1906 an angry crowd repeated the destruction of fences and cottage. G.B. Witts read the Riot Act and in due course eight men were tried at Gloucester Assizes.

The eight men received sentences of up to six months' hard labour for their part in the riot in 1906, later reduced on appeal. Walter Ballinger, a clay-digger at Pilley Brickworks and William Heaven, a haulier, were the last to be released, in October of that year. In this photograph Walter Ballinger and his mother stand in the middle; behind them are Ernest Young, a gardener, who had also been imprisoned, and William Heaven (in bowler hat). With the bicycle is Charles Barrett, who had also been sentenced. At the back on the left is George Townsend, the secretary of the Stalwarts' Committee, who afterwards published a ballad 'The Battle of Leckhampton Hill', to rally support for the cause. The story has a happy ending, however. By 1929 the Quarries Company had gone out of business and Cheltenham Town Council bought the estate, thus securing the freedom for all to walk the land.

'A Cabinet Minister in his shirt sleeves.' On 11 October 1922 the Right Honourable Dr Macnamara, Minister of Labour, inaugurated a new railway spur that was to be laid from Charlton Kings station to the Leckhampton Hill quarries. According to a report in the *Cheltenham Chronicle* he exercised so much vigour that, 'taking off his coat, and rolling up his shirt sleeves, he doubled up the silver presentation spade and had to resort to a common or garden one [with which] he lifted the fine sod he is seen holding in the above picture'. This standard-gauge line was intended to provide a direct outlet for quarry stone via the Great Western Railway. It crossed the Lilleybrook Golf Course and Sandy Lane, and passed beneath a bridge carrying Daisy Bank Road before linking up with the Middle Incline.

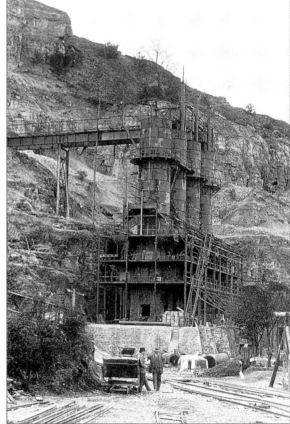

Limekilns under construction in 1924, near the top of the Middle Incline. From the traces that remain today it is hard to envisage the unsightly and noisy industrial development that disfigured the hill until comparatively recently. The four huge steel kilns were 77 feet high. Limestone from the upper workings was fed into the cylinders from the gantry above and the end-product was taken down the hill in wagons towards the rail link at Charlton Kings.

Another view of the limekilns, by now in operation, 1924. They were fired by gas, which was produced on the site from coal.

The stoneyard by the depot at the foot of the hill, in the early 1920s; a site now occupied by the Leckhampton Industrial Estate. Note the tramway entering the works. Twenty workmen and their foreman are on parade for the photograph. They produced stone for building and monumental work, including tombstones for the Imperial War Graves Commission.

Leckhampton Hill from Church Meadow, *c.* 1915. The view today has hardly changed.

The curving lines of ridge and furrow on the slopes of Court Hill in the winter snow, 1979. Leckhampton provides numerous examples of this feature, which is the result of medieval ploughing by teams of oxen. The furrows assisted drainage and, before enclosure and the advent of hedges and ditches, also served to demarcate separate plots of land.

Daisy Bank Pleasure Gardens, 1930s. They were situated at the rear of the bungalow called Underscar and would have been frequented by Cheltenham people who came to the hill for walks and picnics, especially when they could take advantage of the trams or buses to get there.

The slopes of the hill beyond Daisy Bank in the 1930s, before the shacks and bungalows had been built.

Salterley Grange Sanatorium from the air, c. 1930, showing the layout of the chalets, one block for men, the other for women. Salterley Grange was purchased in 1907 by the Birmingham Corporation as a sanatorium for those suffering from tuberculosis (or, as it was still called at that time, consumption) – a chilling reminder of what a scourge the disease was in living memory. The last patient left in 1969 and residential accommodation has now been built on the site. The main house dates from about 1860.

Salterley Grange Sanatorium, men's section, c. 1935. The chalets were designed to enable the patients to obtain as much fresh air as possible, even in midwinter. The patients were not permitted to talk at certain times of the day, when a bell would be rung for silence.

6

The Naunton Park Area

The almshouses, Naunton Park, date unknown. In 1899 twelve cottage homes were built for the aged poor, with a resident nurse, thanks to a bequest of Mr John Alexander Hay and his wife Marianne Louisa.

The entrance gates to Naunton Park, *c.* 1905. The rustic central arch bears the words 'Naunton Park'. The park was opened in 1893 and ornamental gardens and the sports field were developed. Other notable features, which have since disappeared, were a thatched bandstand, an ornate 20-foot high drinking fountain (which can be made out in this photograph) and an avenue of poplar trees. A park-keeper was present during opening times and kept a stern watch on mischievous children; one appears in uniform in the photograph on page 110. A fund-raising group called the Friends of Naunton Park has recently been set up and has made good progress in refurbishing the gardens.

Naunton Park Schools soon after their opening in 1906. They comprised infant, junior and secondary schools, the older boys and girls at first being educated separately. For nearly thirty years until 1950 the headmaster was Arthur Dye, later Mayor of Cheltenham.

Naunton Park teaching staff, 1907. Standing, left to right: Miss Hobley, Miss Kendall, Miss Lane, Mr Ricketts, Miss Croome, Mr Doxey, Miss Penberthy, Mr Skey, Miss Brown, Mr Knee (caretaker), Mr Walker. Seated: Mrs Maybrey, Mr Jarvis, Miss Davis (headmistress of the infants' school), Mr Fenning (headmaster), Miss Routledge (headmistress of the girls' school), Mr Hill, Miss Stone.

Naunton Park School infants' class, 1937. The following children have been identified. Back row: 4th from left Michael Stock, 8th Michael Scarrott. Middle row: 1st and 2nd from left the twins Doreen and Betty Hoare, 6th Jack Potts, 9th Jean Lloyd. Front row: 1st from left Ann Pragnell, 4th Ray Loveridge, 7th Molly Stancombe. Seated on the ground: Ken James, Terry Enoch.

Naunton Park Red Cross Hospital during the First World War. The school was taken over as a hospital for wounded servicemen, in common with several other schools and establishments in the town. The school hall was used as a ward, with doctors, nurses and patients cheerfully posing for the photograph. The hospital was capable of handling over a hundred patients and a plaque records the fact that 2,751 cases were treated between June 1915 and December 1918. In the postcard reproduced above, the Red Cross flag is shown flying and two wounded soldiers have been superimposed, presumably to make it look more like a hospital. The scholars had to go to Leckhampton School instead, where a two-shift system was introduced.

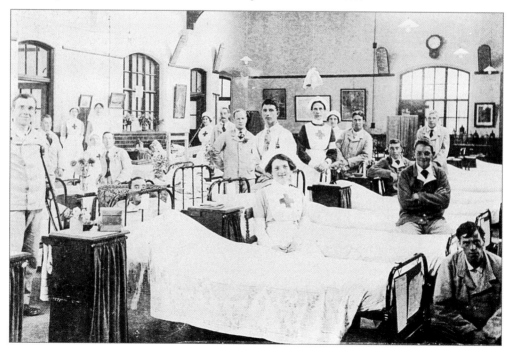

Naunton Park Hospital Fête, with patients parading in decorated wheelchairs. The patients had the exclusive use of the playing field at certain times of the day, and those convalescing formed sports teams, playing against other hospitals in the area.

Naunton Park Road, c. 1910. As is so often the case in photographs of this era, there is a group of small children willing to pose. The East Gloucestershire Croquet Club in Old Bath Road is at the far end. The houses in the middle have been replaced.

Another view of Naunton Park, looking towards Naunton Lane, in the early years of the twentieth century.

The Pilford Garage in Old Bath Road, 1994. Already this is part of history, as the garage closed soon afterwards, being unable to compete with the larger concerns in busier locations. A small group of houses has been built on the site, around Kenneth Close, named after the late Ken Hammond, a town councillor and alderman for many years and mayor in 1980, who lived locally. In the 1940s the garage had been owned by Thomas Little, who offered servicing and repairs and rented private lock-up garages.

7

The Rural Scene

Cows proceeding up Farm Lane towards Leckhampton Farm, 1943. Cummings Cottages can be seen faintly in the distance. The cows were in the charge of a landgirl of the Women's Land Army, one of several who also did the milking and made the deliveries. Others worked in the market gardens around Kidnappers Lane.

Above: Farmer Frederick and Emma Ellis Hicks walking across 'Phelp's Piece', a field on the west side of Farm Lane, *c.* 1909. Below: Leckhampton Farm, with their son Dennis outside, holding his golf clubs. The date is presumably between 1911 and 1922 when the nearby golf club was in business. The porch of the farmhouse later fell down when the ivy was removed! The farm dates back to at least the eighteenth century and was shown by the name of Berry Farm in a parish survey of 1835.

Threshing at Leckhampton Farm in 1941 – the first
crop of corn harvested there since the First World War,
grown on the orders of the Ministry of Agriculture.
Sheepshearing was also carried out on the farm at
that time.

Leckhampton Farm undergoing restoration together with a barn conversion, 1992. The barn bears a stone-cut
plaque dated 1819.

Cummins Row on Farm Lane, *c.* 1908. These three dwellings (listed as Cummings Cottages in the 1891 census) have more recently been modernised as a single residence and named Little Vatch. Note the gate across Farm Lane, which remained in use within living memory, as the field beyond was not fenced off.

Moat Cottage, in snow, 1960. It is of 'cruck' construction, a pair of matching timbers supporting the gable ends. It is probably the oldest cottage in Leckhampton, its deeds dating from the late sixteenth century. Moat Cottage, Sheepshead Row and Field Cottage (now renamed Olde England) lie alongside a track at the heart of the ancient village.

...eorge Bubb, agricultural labourer, hedger and ditcher, ...ate unknown. He is reputed to have had the ability to ...histle and charm birds into perching beside him as he ...orked in the fields.

...till ploughing at the age of seventy-seven: Ted Smith ...ith his horses on the slopes of Leckhampton Hill in ...936. He was a farm labourer all his life, for much of ...he time at Collum End Farm, and did not retire until ...e was eighty. He lived at 48 Pilley Lane.

An aerial view of Leckhampton Farm, in Farm Lane, probably in the 1950s. The barn and the buildings grouped around the farmyard stand out clearly, as do the orchard to the right of the farm and (once again) the ridge and furrow traces of ancient ploughing. Neat rows of hay stooks or wheat sheaves can be seen in the fields to the left. Church Road and Hall Road are in the distance. The area shown is still largely open fields, though under threat of development.

Right: Fred Cotton, on his round, date unknown. He retired in 1928 at the age of seventy-three as Cheltenham's oldest milkman, after fifty-eight years in the employ of Frederick Hicks of Leckhampton and Church Farms. He carried out other tasks on the farm, and other photographs in the Society's possession show him in control of a horse-drawn rake, downing a refreshing drink, and watching a cricket match with his friend George Bubb. Below: Fred's daughter Dot in the smartly painted Church Farm milk float.

Starlight, one of the last horses owned by Leckhampton Dairies, late 1950s. Starlight and its stablemates perished in a fire at the dairy in 1962, to the great regret of local residents whose milk was delivered in carts towed by these patient animals. The dairy then converted to vans and electric floats for its deliveries; it was later taken over by Cheltenham Dairies and in turn by the Cotteswold Dairy.

8

People

Robert Cary Barnard, 1827–1906. His working life was spent in the Army, though he took early retirement with the rank of major in his late thirties. He had great energy and wide interests and was an active member of Cheltenham's scientific and literary societies. His love of Leckhampton and its past led him to transcribe and study the parish records which he wrote about in 1897 in his book *Records of Leckhampton*. His son Leonard was much involved in the life of the village and his grandson Major Tom Barnard, who became a professional artist after his retirement from the Army, also lived in Leckhampton until his recent death.

A game of cards, a drink of cider and a clay pipe, somewhere in Leckhampton, 1909. This seems to be a carefully posed portrait, with the men wearing contrasting styles of hat and rustic attire, against the background of a Cotswold stone wall. Their names were Thomas Baker, Branby White and Will Thompson.

Richard Purser, 'the oldest man in England', in 1868. He died soon after this photograph was taken and is buried in Leckhampton churchyard. The age given on the tombstone is 111. He claimed to have been taken by his mother at the age of four to see 'an illumination in honour of the Coronation of King George III' in 1760. The *Cheltenham Examiner* reported that he had worked as a labourer up to within a few weeks of his death, his scanty earnings being supplemented by an annual grant of £5 from the Crown and by 'occasional gratuities from his wealthier neighbours, who sympathising with his great age felt pleasure in contributing to lightening his burden'.

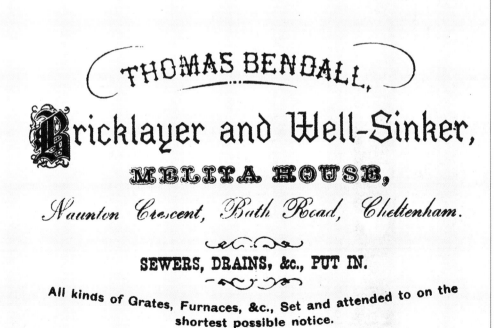

Thomas Bendall, in a bath chair, attended by his daughter Lucy, presumably in the last years before his death in 1913 at the age of eighty-eight. He had lived at his home in Naunton Crescent for fifty years – Melita House, as shown on his trade card, below. As a well-sinker he followed in the footsteps of his father Samuel, who founded his family's fortunes in the area, and as a bricklayer he set the pattern for his son John, who built houses and schools in various parts of Cheltenham.

THOMAS BENDALL,

Bricklayer and Well-Sinker,

MELITA HOUSE,

Naunton Crescent, Bath Road, Cheltenham.

SEWERS, DRAINS, &c., PUT IN.

All kinds of Grates, Furnaces, &c., Set and attended to on the shortest possible notice.

Above: Barnard George Thompson, headmaster of Leckhampton School from 1886 to 1913, and his wife Susan Isabel, photographed in 1908. Barnard Thompson was prominent in the social life of the village, and Thompson Drive is named after him. Below: their daughter Grace as a Red Cross nurse at the Leckhampton Court Hospital during the First World War, and Sidney, their eldest son, when serving in the Boer War in the Imperial Yeomanry. He later joined the 21st Lancers and was killed in action in Belgium at the age of thirty-four, with the rank of acting sergeant-major. His younger brother Ernest, a company quartermaster sergeant in the 1st Grenadier Guards, was killed near Ypres on the following day.

The wedding of Alfred Thomas Bendall and Grace Evelyn Thompson at Leckhampton church, August 1916. Alf was John Bendall's fourth son, on leave as a corporal in the Worcestershire Regiment. John Bendall and his wife Sarah are seated on the left. Alf's brothers Hubert Arthur and John Lionel are standing on the extreme left and third from left respectively and Ian Charles is sitting on the extreme right; his sisters Enid Maud, Freda and Doris are sitting in front. Grace's mother is seated third from the right and her sister Winifred is standing on the extreme right. Alf Bendall later served as a sergeant in Mesopotamia. After the war he gave loyal service to the community and when he died in 1971 at the age of eighty he was described in an obituary as 'the unofficial mayor of Leckhampton'. In this he maintained the family tradition, for his father had been three times mayor of Cheltenham. Alfred and his three brothers all joined their father's building firm. He was president of the Leckhampton Sports Club (see Chapter Nine) and before the war had played rugby for the Cheltenham Town team.

Dr Harold Lloyd-Davies, photographed in probably 1912, aged forty-four. He was a local general practitioner, much loved by his patients and respected and admired by his colleagues. He also worked at the Delancey Hospital and, during the First World War, at the Leckhampton Court Red Cross Hospital. After dealing with many cases of sickness during the postwar influenza epidemic, he himself caught the disease in 1920 and died of pneumonia. He worked from a surgery in his own family home, Italia Villa on the corner of Leckhampton Road and Croft Street. This remained in use until his successors moved to the new surgery named after him in Moorend Park Road.

Domenico Barnett, Professor of Music at the Ladies' College from 1866 until his death in 1911. He was described as a brilliant musician and teacher, who nevertheless 'found it hard to suffer fools gladly' and 'would tear his hair and hurl music on the floor, in agony at his pupils' imperfections', while the clerk in charge of the stationery office acted as a chaperone. He lived at Cliff Cottage, Leckhampton Hill and is buried in Leckhampton churchyard in the same grave as his father, John. John Barnett (1802–90) was also a celebrated musician of his time, who spent fifty years as a singing-master in Cheltenham and is described on his tombstone as 'the father of English opera'. Chief among these now forgotten works was one entitled *A Mountain*

Members of the Capper family, in photographs donated by the late Geoff Capper, a loyal supporter of the Local History Society, who died in 1999. Above: Edmund Capper and his son Charles at a gathering of the Oddfellows Friendly Society in Cheltenham, *c.* 1900. Charles was the father of Geoff Capper and was born in 1875. Edmund was a builder who lived in Moorend Crescent. Right: Clara, daughter of Edmund and Elizabeth Capper, probably *c.* 1890. She worked in Cheltenham as a dressmaker, and had perhaps made the lovely dress she is wearing for the photograph.

J.F. Ballinger, in 1915, at the age of sixty-eight. He had just completed fifty years as verger at Leckhampton church, during which time he had not missed a single Sunday service. He did not give up the position for another ten years. He lived at Gothic Cottage, Moorend Street, at which address in the 1891 census he was described as a gardener.

Anthony Mustoe in 1907, at the age of ninety-three. His address was 12 Moorend Street, where he had lived since his wedding sixty-four years earlier. He was summoned as the oldest witness in the Leckhampton Hill dispute. He recalled that he had helped to build St Luke's church, St Gregory's Roman Catholic church and the Great Western station. He also travelled to London in the first GWR train that ran from Cirencester, walking from Cheltenham in the morning to catch it.

B.C. Enoch in Boy Scout uniform, 1914. He was to continue in the family business as a builder and plumber.

Joe Isaac, who was a farrier in Exmouth Street, with a gate he had fashioned from sixty-nine horseshoes, 1948. He also worked at the racecourse, and many of the shoes used in the gate were racing plates made of aluminium, including several from National Hunt winners. The gate was at 10 Leckhampton Road in 1948 but has since been removed. A blacksmith is still in business at the same premises in Exmouth Street.

A Cheltenham society wedding. Arthur Dale, the son of Mr and Mrs Henry Dale of Daisy Bank House, Leckhampton and Evelyn Laura Cowper Russell, of Charlton Kings, were married at Leckhampton church on 29 April 1915. This photograph shows the bridal group, with relatives, at the reception.

George Backhouse Witts, of Hill House, 1906. G.B. Witts was a leading figure in Leckhampton in his time, a magistrate and the first chairman of the Leckhampton Parish Meeting – later the Rural District Council. He was a great friend of his neighbour, R.C. Barnard, sharing his interest in local history and in the campaign for free access to the hill. He was an entertaining speaker and was known to follow a lecture on the geology of Leckhampton Hill by singing some Gloucestershire ballads, while on another occasion he illustrated a talk on natural science with some 'experiments of quite a startling character'.

Thomas William Smith, haulier and builder, with his horses and workers in Naunton Parade, *c*. 1900. His grandson Albert sits on the horse in the centre. The worker on the right is Jim Whitfield.

Pupils of St Philip's School in Leckhampton Road, 1906. B.C. Enoch (*see* p. 99) is on the second row up, second from left.

Dr Edward J. Wilson MB FRCP, father of
Dr Edward A. Wilson, the Antarctic explorer,
1899. Dr Wilson, senior, was a doctor at
Cheltenham General and the Delancey
Hospitals. Below: The Crippetts, 1886. The
previous year Mrs Wilson had taken a tenancy
on the house with a view to farming the land.
It was at The Crippetts that Edward Wilson
developed his love and knowledge of nature
and art, while a day boy at Cheltenham
College. In the foreground on the left is a pond
which in 1890 Edward Wilson helped to clear
of weeds, nearly drowning when he later took
a swim in it.

A family group, showing Edward Wilson (bottom left) with his father and mother in the centre, his sisters and the Rendall brothers. It is dated 1886, when Edward was fourteen. His sister Lilian is standing at the back of the group; ten years later she married Bernard Rendall (seated at the front, with tennis racket). After reading medicine and natural sciences at Cambridge, Edward was in due course appointed as chief of the scientific staff in Captain Scott's expedition to the Antarctic, where he was able to put his artistic skills to good purpose. He died with Captain Scott and three other companions on the return journey, having reached the South Pole. A room in Cheltenham Museum contains memorabilia from that expedition, including some examples of his sketchbooks and paintings.

Robert Hunt with his grandfather, Robert Cotton, sometime landlord of the Malvern Inn, in about 1930. One of Leckhampton's most distinguished sons, Robert Hunt was one of the first engineering apprentices to be taken on by George Dowty in 1935. He was later to gain a knighthood, as chairman and chief executive of the Dowty Group following Sir George's death. His grandfather had been a considerable entrepreneur and landowner in Leckhampton. He had had the Malvern Inn built and moved into it from Gritmore Cottage. Letitia Kirkham, who is shown as licensee of the Malvern Inn in a photograph on page 56, was his sister.

Bruce Stait, 1928–95, one of the founders of the Leckhampton Local History Society. Several of the photographs in this book are from his extensive collection and include some which he himself took from the air in the 1960s as a passenger in a light aircraft piloted by a member of the Rotol Flying Club, based at Staverton. Bruce came to Cheltenham in 1952 to work in the Rotol drawing office and in 1990 wrote the authoritative history of that company. He was on the committee of the Skyfame Museum at Staverton and took an active interest in the restoration of historic aircraft. He also had a great interest in the history of the Cheltenham area and led guided walks as a Cotswold warden.

A visit by Lady Ryder to the Leckhampton Court Sue Ryder Home for Palliative Care in probably 1980. The Mayors of Cheltenham and Tewkesbury are present (on the left and right respectively), and James Graham, Chairman of the Leckhampton Parish Council, is at the back on the right.

Prince Charles, together with Lady Ryder, at the opening of the day care unit at Leckhampton Court in 1992. The Prince is patron of the home and takes a personal interest in its affairs. The day unit is in 'Goose Bay', originally the stable block. Princess Diana paid a visit in 1984.

A Leckhampton Parish Council meeting in Alf Bendall's front room, probably in the late 1950s. Standing, left to right: Alf Bendall, Mr Oakey, Mr Hipkiss, Mr T.A.D. Clark, Mr Harrison. Sitting: Fred Tibbles, Mrs Mollie Clark, -?-, Jack Sweet, -?-.

Canon Henry Proctor, who was the incumbent priest at St Peter's from 1904 to 1912. His aims were to raise the spiritual tone of the parish and to involve the laity more actively. He fought vigorously for Church of England control over the enlarged village school in 1906. He was given to making stoical quotations, such as 'whom the Lord loveth, He chasteneth' and he disapproved of carol-singing at the doors of houses, since 'besides being too often grossly irreverent and even blasphemous, it begets in them the demoralising habit of begging'. He often carried a walking stick, black with silver mounting, which he was apt to leave behind absent-mindedly after visiting a parishioner.

9

Sports & Leisure

Leckhampton cricket team, 1914. The following have been identified. Back row, left to right: -?-, -?-, G. Wilson Fenning (the Leckhampton schoolmaster), G. Seymour, W. Seymour, L. Harley (scorer). Middle row: Bill Allen, the Revd F.W. Bidwell, Ernie Palmer (captain), J. Bendall, -?-. Front row: -?-, -?-, W. Townsend.

Leckhampton Cricket Club, 1898. Standing, left to right: the Revd Clifford Aston (president), S.B. Thompson, W. Chick, J. Shill, W. Coates (captain), H. Chick, Opie Hayden, P. Herbert, Barnard G. Thompson (honorary secretary), E.J. Murphy, F. Caudle (umpire). Seated: Theo Pearman, F. Tilling, D. Coates, W.H. Caudle (scorer).

It is interesting to see the presence of the parish priest Clifford Aston and the village schoolmaster Barnard Thompson. During this season the team played fourteen matches, with Clifford Aston heading the batting averages. Opposing sides included the Gordon League, the Married Men, British Old Boys, Vulcan Iron Works, the Gas Works, the Police, Steel's XI, Cavendish XI, Pilley Temperance, St James's Institute and Charlton Kings. The teams played on a ground in Charlton Lane.

The Emmanuel Football Team, 1923, which played in Division III of the Cheltenham and District League.

Leckhampton Football Club, 1920.

Leckhampton Football First Team, with officials and supporters, 1921/22. Back row, left to right: R. Holdsworth, J. Charlton, H.H. Rogers (secretary), J. Charlton, J.L. Bendall. Third row: J.E. Youlds, H.S. Marshall, F. Aldridge, T. Bassett, J. Preece, P. Allen, the Revd F.R. Standfast, J.E. Palmer (referee), E.J. Fletcher. Second row: F. Fisher, H.A. Bendall, S.S. Bendall, H.J. Bendall (captain), H. Payne, J.H. Moss, J.D. Bendall. Front row: A. Bendall, W. Wakefield.

Naunton Park Rugby Football Club, 1908/9, together with (opposite) a fixture list from the following season. The picture was taken in the park, with the thatched shelter in the background. The captain in the centre is Gilbert Clark, and John Lionel Bendall and Alf Bendall are also present, seated, while J.D. Bendall is standing at the back, third from left. The gentleman at the extreme left, wearing a forbidding uniform of Teutonic appearance, is the park-keeper Mr Sutton. Standing at the extreme right is Mr W.J. Price (honorary secretary, according to the fixture card), with his son sitting beside him. Mr Price was reputedly 'the last town crier of Cheltenham'. The long and august list of vice-presidents on the fixture card – Lord Duncannon, the Mayor of Cheltenham, the Member of Parliament, the Principal of Cheltenham College, the Rector of Cheltenham, Dr Lloyd-Davies, as well as other councillors, solicitors and clerical gentlemen – implies that the club must have carried some prestige. Out of twenty-one matches, played against respectable teams from a wide area, it lost only two and drew two.

NAUNTON PARK (RUGBY)
FOOTBALL CLUB.
SEASON 1909-1910.

PRESIDENT:
Major P. G. Shewell.

VICE-PRESIDENTS:
Lord Duncannon,
Major Peake, Major Rickerby.
J. E. Sears, Esq., M.P., J.P.,
W. Nash Skillicorne, Esq., J.P.,
The Mayor of Cheltenham, J. T. Agg-Gardner,
Esq., J.P.
Aldermen J. B. Winterbotham G. Norman, and
R. Rogers,
The Principal of Cheltenham College, the
Rev. R. Waterfield, M.A.,
The Rector of Cheltenham, the
Rev. F. L'Estrange Fawcett M.A.
Rev. A. C. Woodhouse. M.A., Rev. H. E. Noot, M.A.
Rev. M. Tanner, M.A., Dr. Lloyd Davies,
Councillors J. D. Bendall, R. Steel, C. H. Margrett,
H. Stroud, H. G. Norton, and T. H. Packer.

C. Brown, Esq., C.I.E.	C. Hall, Esq.
J. Barton, Esq.	F. F. Handley, Esq.
P. R. Clauss, Esq.	Hylton Jessop, Esq.
J. E. Bendall, Esq.	A. S. F. Pruen, Esq.
C. Dickins, Esq.	J. Player, Esq.
T. Fitzroy Fenwick, Esq.	E. D. Ricketts, Esq.

VICE-PRESIDENTS (continued):

L. Sharp, Esq.	W. J. Moore. Esq.
W. Sawyer, Esq.	R. C. Monk. Esq.
F. Stroud, Esq.	T. Norman. Esq.
R. E. Steel, Esq.	R. Ticehurst. Esq.
A. G. Taynton Esq.	T. Wilkins. Esq.
E. W. Moore, Esq.	H. Winning. Esq.

R. Earl Marshall. Esq.
Messrs. J. M. Bellamy, F. Goulding, F. J. Pearce,
and J. H. Evans.

CAPTAIN: Mr. J. T. Bendall.
SUB-CAPTAIN: Mr. R. McArthur.

COMMITTEE:

A. C. Carter.	W. J Price.
F. Goulding.	F. Read.
J. A. Ingram.	J. Sutton.
Ray Norman.	H. Sheen.
W. Norman.	F. Tovey.
J. H. Newman.	E. Wright.
F. J. Pearce.	A. C. Varnish.

HON. TREASURER:
Councillor J. D. Bendall.
Home Orchard, Church Road, Leckhampton.

HON. SECRETARY:
Mr. W. J. Woodhouse,
1, Croft Villas, Leckhampton, Cheltenham.

HON. TEAM SECRETARY:
Mr. G. A. Clark,
83, Naunton Crescent, Cheltenham.

CLUB COLOURS: Green and Black Hoops.

FIXTURES, SEASON 1909-1910.

Date.	OPPONENTS.	Where Played.	Result.
1909 Sept. 11	Practice	Home ...	—
,, 18	Town v. District	Away ...	
,, 25	Cotswold	Away ...	W
Oct. 2	Bristol Imperial	Away ...	W
,, 9	Tredworth	Away ...	
,, 16	Cheltenham "A"	Away ...	W
,, 23	Gordon League	Away ...	W
,, 30	Moseley Harlequins	Home ...	W
Nov. 6	Moseley Harlequins	Away ...	
,, 13	R.A. College	Away ...	W
,, 20	St. Paul's	Home ...	W
,, 27	Bath "A"	Home ...	
Dec. 4	Swindon Engineering College ...	Away ...	W
,, 11	Glo'ster Old Boys	Home ...	W
,, 18	Bath "A"	Away ...	W
,, 27	Cheltenham "A"	Home ...	
1910. Jan. 1	Tredworth	Home ...	W
,, 8	Territorials	Home ...	
,, 15	St. Paul's	Away ...	W
,, 22	Stow-on-the-Wold	Home ...	W
,, 29	Swindon Engineering College ...	Home ...	W
Feb. 5	Glo'ster Old Boys	Away ...	D
,, 12	Gordon League	Home ...	W
,, 19	Territorials	Away ...	
,, 26	R A. College	Home ...	D
Mar. 5	Stow-on-the-Wold	Away ...	
,, 12	Bristol Imperial	Home ...	D
,, 19	Cheltenham "A"	Home ...	W
,, 26	Newport Extras	Home ...	W

Naunton Park Rugby Football Club, 1922. The team was still a force to be reckoned with. This photograph was taken on the occasion when it defeated the previously unbeaten Old Patesians. Standing, left to right: – Allen, J. Wilson, C.C. Channon (team secretary), A.E. Carey, W.H. Pears, ? Kilminster, S.E. Harding, -?-, S. Alsbury, -?-, C. Taylor, ? Holloway, H. Sheen. Seated: C. Powell, A. Bendall, A. Green, J. Voyce, H.W. Hall (captain), W. Sly, N. Powell, H.R. Symonds. Front row: H.A. Bendall and C. Goldthorpe.

St Philip's Quoits Club, 1901. Quoits was a popular game at that period and the Pilley team would have played against others in the area, such as the St Stephen's Cricket and Quoits Club. The Leckhampton Lads' Club also played in the 1920s. It is interesting to speculate on the purpose of the shovel!

The New Miniature Rifle Club for Ladies at Leckhampton, at its opening meeting in 1909. The range is seen at the right of the picture and was situated at the back of the Working Men's Club (now Old Farthings), where the ladies (described in a newspaper article as 'shootettes') practised on two afternoons a week. The ladies represented many of the influential local families. Back row, left to right: Mr Cotton (instructor), Mr Little (president of the men's club), Mrs Ward*, Miss Thompson, Miss Walker, Mrs W. Sharpe, Miss Whishaw, Miss Hicks, Mrs Hicks, Miss Hopkins, Mrs Meredith, Miss Douglas, Mrs Robertson, Mrs Hopkins, Miss Cross, Miss Maitland Reid, Mrs Milligan, Miss Bourne*. Front row: Miss Barnard*, Miss Ethel Smith*, Lady Winterbotham*, Mrs Boyd Cardew*, Mrs Elwes (president), Miss Wood*, Miss Hargreaves*. (* = committee)

Local children at play in the flooded sandpits off Sandy Lane in 1941. This is now the Old Patesians' sports ground. The children are Clive Taylor, Sid Abbott, David Blunt, Roy Abbott and Hiram Lockwood.

The North Gloucestershire Golf Club, which was in existence from 1911 to 1922. The top picture shows the clubhouse (now a private house) near the corner of Leckhampton Lane and Crippetts Lane. The bottom picture is a view of the course looking across to the hill with Crippetts Lane in the middle distance. Sheep grazing on the course provided an additional hazard. The house marked with a cross is Ferncliffe, where the writer of the postcard was staying. In 1914 an exhibition match was played on the course by the English champion, Henry Vardon, and an ex-champion, Ted Ray, watched by a large crowd. Ray set a record for the course of sixty-two strokes. The club closed in 1915 on account of the war and reopened in 1919 with a nine-hole course (advertised as being 'on excellent golfing turf, and not in the least of a strenuous character') but it finally closed in 1922, having been eclipsed by the Cleeve Hill and Lilleybrook clubs.

Liddington Lake Pleasure Gardens, *c.* 1905. Situated around some flooded clay pits near Leckhampton station, these grounds opened in 1893 but eventually lost popularity and closed in 1911. In their heyday people flocked there from miles around, first on foot and then by tram, the record attendance being 2,300 visitors on Easter Monday 1897. The lake offered fishing, swimming, canoes and rowing boats for hire, rides on steamers (named *Pioneer* and *Mayflower*), and skating in winter. Programmes of sports and prize competitions were arranged, there were side shows, swings and slides, and band concerts and dancing were popular attractions. The refreshment house – Liddington itself, which served teas and temperance drinks – alone remains, now occupied by the office of a construction company.

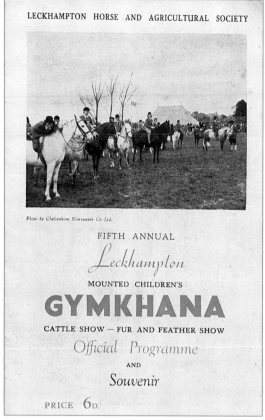

LECKHAMPTON HORSE AND AGRICULTURAL SOCIETY

Photo by Cheltenham Newspaper Co. Ltd.

FIFTH ANNUAL

Leckhampton

MOUNTED CHILDREN'S

GYMKHANA

CATTLE SHOW — FUR AND FEATHER SHOW

Official Programme

AND

Souvenir

PRICE 6D.

The cover of the programme for the Leckhampton Children's Gymkhana and Cattle, Fur and Feather Show held on 10 April 1950 at Burrows Sports Ground. These events were very popular, as is shown in the photograph below, taken probably at the 1946 show. Terry Enoch is the boy in the centre of the picture, sporting a cap. In earlier times, until the mid-1930s, the 'Village Fête and Monster Fair' used to be held in the grounds of the court, hosted by Mrs Elwes. There were usually running races, a tug-of-war, donkey polo, a tent-pegging competition, and 'pig-sticking' on ponies, for prizes such as five hundredweight of coal, a leg of mutton, a duck, rabbits and corn.

Valerie Singleton at the Scout Fête on the school playing field in 1968. Val was then the presenter of the popular children's TV programme *Blue Peter* and had been invited as guest of honour to open the show.

Leckhampton Girls' Club, 1909, in a photograph taken by Frank Webley. Grace Thompson, the mother of Jean Bendall, is second from the right on the back row. The group probably belong to the Girls' Drill Club, which was formed in 1909 under the leadership of Miss C.S. Barnard and Miss H. Bourne. Some of the girls are holding the dumb-bells (or possibly the 'bat-bells') which they used in public displays, as well as wands and Indian clubs. They also practised country dancing and dancing round a maypole. Their uniform was a white blouse, a blue slip and a red belt.

A walking race from Birdlip to Cheltenham was held in 1902. This photograph shows the leader of the race passing down Leckhampton Road, accompanied by several cyclists.

The bonfire on Leckhampton Hill to celebrate Queen Victoria's Golden Jubilee in 1887. Considerable effort evidently went into its construction, the elaborate framework being necessary to support the 30-foot high pile of brushwood. An even taller bonfire was built on the hill for the Diamond Jubilee.

The celebration of the Coronation of King Edward VII on 9 August 1902. In this photograph we see the local children enjoying a 'meat tea', after playing games in the field behind the school house. The day had begun with a service in the church, and at 2 o'clock all parishioners of the age of the King upwards (i.e. sixty years and over) had sat down to a dinner served in the parish hall. At 6.30 p.m. Mrs G.B. Witts planted an oak tree outside the hall to commemorate the Coronation, and in the evening there was dancing and 'kiss-in-the-ring', with fairy lights decorating the trees at the entrance to the field.

The programme for Leckhampton's celebrations for the Coronation of King George V, 22 June 1911. The events followed a well-established pattern, culminating in the lighting of a bonfire on Leckhampton Hill.

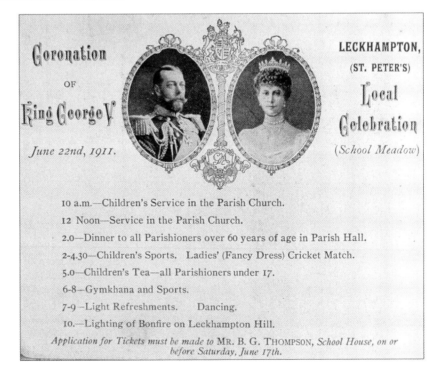

Coronation

OF

King George V

June 22nd, 1911.

LECKHAMPTON,

(ST. PETER'S)

Local Celebration

(School Meadow)

10 a.m.—Children's Service in the Parish Church.

12 Noon—Service in the Parish Church.

2.0—Dinner to all Parishioners over 60 years of age in Parish Hall.

2-4.30—Children's Sports.   Ladies' (Fancy Dress) Cricket Match.

5.0—Children's Tea—all Parishioners under 17.

6-8—Gymkhana and Sports.

7-9—Light Refreshments.   Dancing.

10.—Lighting of Bonfire on Leckhampton Hill.

Application for Tickets must be made to MR. B. G. THOMPSON, *School House, on or before Saturday, June 17th.*

Some of the performers in the Leckhampton pantomime *The Pied Piper of Hamelin*, outside the parish hall, Januar
1920. This pantomime was one of several written and performed by enthusiastic amateurs around that tim
Elaborate programmes, including the full scripts, have survived from the productions of 1910 and 1911, whe
L.W. Barnard and Miss C.S. Barnard ('Barnards Unlimited') put on *The King of the Golden River* and *The Princess ar
the Goblins*. The performers were members of the Church Lads' Brigade and the Girls' Club, which the Barnarc
helped to organise. The readers of the parish magazine were encouraged to attend the 'Theatre Roya
Leckhampton' in preference to 'that other village known as Cheltenham'. Today the Leckhampton Player
founded in 1947, vigorously follow this tradition.

The cast of *Rumpelstiltskin* on the stage of the parish hall, 1922. The main roles were played by B.C. Enoch (Lord Never Saydie), Alf Bendall (Napoo the Tester), H. Bendall (King Stoneybroke of Lackington), C. Richings (Lord Dismal Doldrum). Miss F. Bendall (Duchess of Comme-il-faut) and Miss D. Cotton (Rumpelstiltskin). 'Lackington' was an historic alternative name for the village, evidently still in informal use in the 1920s.

The Leckhampton Women's Institute was formed in 1947. The top photograph shows members of a fruit canning team at work in the parish hall. In the lower photograph, a larger group poses outside. Back row, left to right: Mrs Manson, Mrs Eve Fordham, Mrs Morewood. Middle row: Mrs Harrison, Mrs Evans, Miss Griffiths, Mrs Griffiths. Front row: Mrs Noble, Mrs Doris Yeend, Mrs Mollie Clarke, Mrs Gwen Sheward, Mrs Oakey. Mrs Clarke (née Cotton) was for many years the president of the Leckhampton branch of the WI. Leaning against the wall behind is a ladies' bicycle, with a string skirt-guard over the rear wheel.

The opening of Burrow's Sports Ground, September 1930. This was provided for the staff of the publishing firm
Ed. J. Burrow and Co. A large pavilion was erected with accommodation for men and women and equipped with
hot and cold baths. Provision was made for cricket, football, running, tennis and other games. The upper picture
shows the pavilion and the marquee ready for the ceremonial opening by the Mayor of Cheltenham, the lower one
part of the crowd. The ground was later taken over by Cheltenham Borough Council.

10

The Second World War

The ruins of Pilley Bridge after the bombing raid on 11 December 1940. Several buildings in Leckhampton were also hit on that occasion, while Cheltenham itself received 2,000 incendiary bombs and 155 high-explosive bombs, resulting in 23 dead, 75 injured, and 600 homeless. Pilley Bridge was the last war-damaged bridge to be repaired in the whole of Great Britain. Legal complications delayed reconstruction until June 1955, and in the meantime a temporary foot-bridge was laid across the railway cutting. More photographs as well as local inhabitants' recollections of this period are included in the Local History Society's book *Leckhampton in the Second World War*.

Leckhampton Home Guard platoon outside the parish hall on 30 May 1942. Back row, left to right: H. Bliss D. Powell, K. Sallis, J. Pollard, W. Bolton, F. Sylvester, H. Cook, E. Machin, H. Symonds, A. Clifford, S. Greening N. Barrett, C. Boddington. Middle row: J. Merrett, N. Preece, F. Weaver, H. Wells, W. Jones, I. Monk, F. Read Seated: W. Hinds, W. Critchley, H. Jeanes, CSM H. Jones, Lieutenant G.L. Heawood, 2nd Lieutenant W.G. Neat R. Wasley, H. Marsh, D. Jones. Lieutenant Heawood was the headmaster of Cheltenham Grammar School and Horace Cook was a teacher at Leckhampton Primary School. One of the platoon's tasks was to guard the bridge over the Kingham railway line as it passed through the district.

he 'Welcome Home' party for Wilfred Townsend outside the parish hall, 1945, after his release from four years
s a prisoner of war in Germany. (Note the grass in front of the building, now covered with tarmac for car
arking.) With the help of local residents, some of whom are shown in a younger guise in this much treasured
hotograph, it has been possible to identify all but one of those present. Front row, left to right: Don Biddle, David
ackson, Hubert Townsend, Agnes Townsend, Wilfred Townsend, Mrs Green, Win Chick (nursing Jennifer), Bert
uise, Billy Brown, William Brown. Second row: Gwen Townsend, Martha Brown (holding Margaret), Miss Coote,
aphne Eeles (with Joan Jackson in front of her), Lily Chick, Margaret Townsend, Violet Guise, Mrs Nottingham,
eggy Hawker. Third row: Mrs Bailey, Geoffrey Nicholls, Mrs Holdsworth, Mary Eeles, Jean Bailey, Eve Fordham,
dith Eeles, Mr Jackson, Mrs Nicholls, Brenda White, -?-, Mrs Jackson, Joyce Ralph. Back row: Mrs Owen, David
runsdon, Mrs White, Jean Bailey, Mrs Brunsdon, Arthur Chick.

Residents of Southern Road and Pilford Road at their VJ Day Celebrations, 15 August 1945. The King's speech was relayed through loudspeakers and there was a 'ceremonial' burning of an effigy of the Emperor of Japan. The following have been identified: Mrs Gomersall, Mr J. Holyoake, Mrs Bennett, Mr Gardner, Mr Bennett, Mrs Bawden, Mrs Wainwright, Mr Jacobs, Mrs Enoch, Mrs Jacobs, Les Roebuck, Mrs Cole, Mrs Holyoake, Miss Edmonds, Mr Stone, Mrs Bethell, Mrs Challis, Mr Cole, Mr Foster, Susan Bennett, Robin Roebuck, John Cole, Terry Enoch, Jeremy Seavers, Colin Wainwright, Colin Gomersall, Mr Hobbs, Mr Challis, Jenny Seavers, Sheila Macfarlane, Valerie Enoch.

he base of one of the wartime Nissen huts erected in the grounds of Leckhampton Court. This recent photograph
rves as a reminder of the period when the court was requisitioned by the War Office. British troops were
ationed there first and later US servicemen arrived, to prepare for the D-Day landings. The huts offered spartan
irroundings for the Americans, many of whom were eventually billeted with local families, with whom they were
ade to feel very much at home. From 1945 to 1948 the huts housed German prisoners of war, who were being
eld for screening and political re-education prior to repatriation. Mostly they worked on farms, and some helped
pair roads or felled timber. In their spare time they played football against local teams, while others formed an
rchestra. Near their skittle alley and chapel they constructed a small fountain, which has recently been re-
ected. In 1947 a party of volunteers refurbished the parish hall, the camp band providing music at the social
ening held to celebrate the completion of the work.

ACKNOWLEDGEMENTS

The photographs and other illustrations in this book are largely supplied by individual members of the Leckhampton Local History Society and other well-wishers. We acknowledge in particular the contributions or assistance of Mrs P.N. Arkell, Mr Bernard Avery, Miss Mary Barker, Mr Arthur Bendall, the late Miss Jean Bendall, Mr David Bick, Mr Don Biddle, the late Mr Geoff Capper, Mr David Cox, Mr Henry Elwes, Mr Terry Enoch, Mr David Hanks, Ms Elaine Heasman, Mr Nigel Hunt, Mr Rick Kedge, Mr John Keen, Mrs Joan Launchbury, Miss Joy Lloyd-Davies, Mr David Lyall, Mrs Barbara Madams, Mrs Maureen Mathias, Mr David Maughfling, Mr Geoff North, Mrs Daphne Oliver, Mr B. Parker, Mr C.W. Purser, Mrs Tacina Rae-Smith, Mr John Randall, Mrs June Stait, Mrs Helen Taylor, Mr Edgar Townsend, Mr Derek Webb, Mrs Betty Wiggins and Mrs Daphne Wheeler. We also thank Mrs Margaret Miller for her help in proofreading.

We acknowledge the assistance provided by the following institutions, which have granted permission to reproduce material held by them: Cheltenham Art Gallery and Museum (in particular Steven Blake), the Gloucestershire Library Service (in particular Roger Beacham and the staff of the Cheltenham Local Studies Library), the *Gloucestershire Echo* (regarding photographs which appeared in that newspaper and in the *Chronicle and Graphic*), The Cheltenham Ladies' College (Mrs Janet Johnstone, Archivist) and the National Monuments Record Centre, Swindon.

Every effort has been made to trace the copyright holders of the photographs used in this book, and any omissions are unintentional. We apologise if there are any errors in the captions. Readers are requested to notify us, care of the Local History Society, of any corrections, or if they have any further information or identifications, or more photographs, which could perhaps be used in a later publication.

SELECT BIBLIOGRAPHY

The sources are to be found chiefly in the Local History Society's own publications but also include:

The Records of Leckhampton, R. Cary Barnard, 1897

Souvenir of Leckhampton Court V.A. Hospital, ed. Sidney Harrison, 1919

In the Days of Miss Beale, F. Cecily Steadman, 1931

Edward Wilson, Nature Lover, George Seaver, 1937

A History of Cheltenham, Gwen Hart, 1965

Cheltenham's Trams and Buses Remembered, John B. Appleby, 1973

The Buildings of England: Gloucestershire, ed. David Verey, 1980

Leckhampton through the Ages, Eve Andrew and Eric Brewin, 1984

Leckhampton within Living Memory, Leckhampton WI, 1957 (unpublished)

The History of Leckhampton Church, Eric Miller, 1989

Old Leckhampton, David Bick, 1994

Leaving All that was Dear, Joe Devereux and Graham Sacker, 1997

An Historical Gazetteer of Cheltenham, James Hodsdon, 1997

A Brief History of Naunton Park, Ann Gibson, 1998